PKY

A.R. 4.1

P+s. 0.5

D1224017

FOOTBALL

FOOTBALL: EQUIPMENT

BRYANT LLOYD

The Rourke Book Co., Inc.
Vero Beach, Florida 32964

EDITORIAL SERVICES:
Penworthy Learning Systems

Library of Congress Cataloging-in-Publication Data

Lloyd, Bryant. 1942
    Football: equipment / by Bryant Lloyd.
        p. cm. — (Football)
    Includes index
    Summary: Describes the equipment and supplies used in football, including the ball, uniforms, helmets, pads, and cleats.
        ISBN 1-55916-212-0 (alk. paper)
        1. Football—Equipment and supplies—Juvenile literature. [1. Football—Equipment and supplies.] I. Title II. Series
    GV950.7.L52 1997
    796.332'028—dc21   97–766
                                                         CIP
                                                         AC

Printed in the USA

TABLE OF CONTENTS

FOOTBALL EQUIPMENT

Football players in full uniform look like knights prepared for war. A helmet covers a player's head and a mask hides his face. Huge shoulder pads bulge under his **jersey** (JER zee).

Football is not war, but it is a rough, hard-hitting game. The players' equipment helps protect them.

The game of football itself requires equipment, too. The most important piece of game equipment is the football.

Colleges and universities with football teams belong to either the National Collegiate Athletic Association (NCAA) or the National Association of Intercollegiate Athletics (NAIA). The NCAA is divided into four levels of competition.

Football players wear equipment to help protect them from injuries.

THE FOOTBALL

A football is the odd duck of game balls. Instead of being round, like a baseball or golf ball, it is shaped like a long egg. It is about 11 inches (28 centimeters) long. The center of the ball is about 7 inches (18 centimeters) around.

Leather pieces make up a football. Today's footballs are more egg-shaped than the football's of the early 1900's.

With its special shape, a football flies neatly through the air and fits snugly against a ball carrier's arm.

The outer layer of professional, college, and high school footballs is made of four leather pieces. Stitches keep the pieces together. A rubber lining inside the leather shell holds air. A football weighs about 15 ounces (425 grams).

GOAL POSTS

The goal posts on college and high school football fields stand on the **end lines** (END LYNZ). A crossbar 10 feet (3 meters) high connects the posts.

High school goal posts are 20 feet (6 meters) high. They are 23 feet 4 inches (7 meters) apart.

College and pro goal posts are 30 feet (9 meters) tall and 18 feet 6 inches (about 5-1/2 meters) apart.

A ball kicked above the crossbar and between the posts can score a **field goal** (FEELD gol) or **extra point** (EK struh POINT).

Goal posts stand on the end line of this football field for players of elementary school age.

THE KICKING TEE

A kicking tee is a small, lightweight support for the football. The tee holds the football in a tilted, upright position on the ground.

Place kickers use a kicking tee for kickoffs. The kicker runs toward the tee and boots the football from it.

Kicking tees have their limits. Wind may knock the football from the tee. Kickers may then have a teammate hold the football in place.

A less physical game of football can be played with pieces of cloth called "flags." A play ends when a defensive player pulls the flag from the belt or pocket of the ball carrier.

Kicking tee supports the football in proper position for the kicker.

THE PLAYER'S EQUIPMENT

Certain safety **gear** (GEER) is basic for everyone who plays tackle football. Not all players, however, wear exactly the same equipment.

Every player wears a helmet. Some players, though, wear more pads than others. Linemen may wear extra padding because they are almost always blocking or tackling other players.

Helmets are extremely important for protection when football players crash into each other or the ground.

Padding inside the helmet usually protects players from serious head injuries.

Running backs, quarterbacks, and defensive backs wear less padding. They need a greater range of arm and leg movement.

THE HELMET

When football was first played in the late 1800's, no one wore a helmet. Many players, over the years, were badly hurt because their heads were not protected.

Today helmets are an extremely important and useful part of a player's equipment. Helmets help protect players from serious head injuries. No one should ever play tackle football without a helmet.

Helmets have a face mask to help protect the eyes and nose. They may also have a mouthguard attached to protect teeth and gums.

Football began about 1850 as a game much like soccer. In the first modern football game, Harvard played McGill in 1874.

Modern helmet, with face mask, mouthguard, and chin strap, was unknown to early football players.

PADS

No amount of equipment can guarantee a player's safety. Helmets and football pads, however, protect players from many injuries.

Shoulder pads cover shoulders and the upper chest and back. Hip pads strap along the sides of the upper legs. Thigh and knee pads also help protect legs. Some players wear arm and elbow pads. Many players wear gloves.

Pads fit under a football player's jersey and pants.

SHOES

Football shoes are commonly called **cleats** (KLEETS). Cleats are the knobs on the bottom of the shoes. Cleats help a player's feet grip the playing field.

Football cleats help players' shoes grip the playing field.

Cleats allow running backs to turn and stop quickly.

Players can choose different types of cleats for different field surfaces. Cleats made for real grass are not as useful on **synthetic** (sin THET ik) grass fields.

Some football shoes are high-tops. They support a player's ankles. Low-cut shoes are popular among running backs, who make quick turns.

UNIFORMS

A player's outer uniform includes a shirt, or jersey, and pants. A number appears on the back and front of the jersey. Sometimes the player's name also appears on the back.

The number and name help game officials and fans identify the player.

The home teams usually wear light colored jerseys. Their pants may be dark or light. Visiting players wear dark jerseys and light or dark pants.

After a kickoff travels just 10 yards (9 meters), it is a free ball. Either team—offense of defense—can recover the ball.

Name and number allow fans, coaches, and officials to tell one player quickly from another.

GLOSSARY

cleats (KLEETS) — the hard knobs on the bottom of football shoes; the shoes themselves

end lines (END LYNZ) — the white lines marking each end of a football field

extra point (EK struh POINT) — the one or two points that the offensive team can make immediately after a touchdown; a conversion

field goal (FEELD gol) — a kick over the crossbar and between the goal posts resulting in three points

gear (GEER) — equipment

jersey (JER zee) — a pullover shirt

synthetic (sin THET ik) — made by people rather than nature

Football players use huge amounts of sticky white tape to support wrists, fingers, ankles, and knees. This player has his shoes taped for a tighter fit and more support.

INDEX